A mid-thirteenth-century illustration of an armourer beating a helm into shape, while a swordsmith checks a blade. Note the mail-covered warhorse.

flat sheet. Large special shears for cutting metal were then used to cut the rough shape. The steel was beaten to the correct shape over an anvil or over smaller, mushroom-headed anvils called stakes. The metal was either worked cold or heated in a furnace to the exact temperature required. Afterwards, the edge might be turned over a length of wire to remove any sharpness. The surface was smoothed by grinding, and then polished. Rivets, leather straps and buckles, as well as linings, were added.

Swords carried a certain mystique, partly because the smiths often kept their methods secret. Early blades were made by twisting iron rods and forging them together, the constant folding and beating leaving a pattern on the smooth metal. These were called pattern-welded blades. Steel was added to increase hardness and sharpness to the more supple iron. Heated blades were plunged into a cold liquid, such as oil or water, to help the hardening process. A wooden or horn grip might be added. This was often bound in cloth, leather or wire to help give a secure grip.

Armour Decoration
Early helmets were decorated with jewels, or were painted. In the fourteenth century a few plate armour pieces had pieces of decorative brass added. By the 1400s, some pieces were engraved by scratching on a design with a sharp instrument called a burin. At the end of the fifteenth century, etching with mild acid had become the main way to decorate armour. Gold was mixed with dangerous mercury that was chased off by heating to leave the gold sealed on the armour.

ARMING A KNIGHT

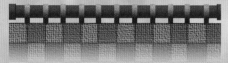

Race Against Time
With the arming doublet in place it took two assistants as little as five minutes to arm a knight – and even less time to remove the armour.

A suit of fifteenth-century plate armour was designed for maximum movement and maximum protection. Plates moved with one another in three ways. Some plates were connected by leather straps riveted on the inner side, some pivoted around a rivet, and a few gave extra movement as the rivet in one plate slid along a slot in the next plate.

An arming doublet was worn under plate armour. This was like a civilian jacket but had mail panels under each armpit and down the inside of the arm to fill the gaps between the plates. The doublet also had strong laces attached to it for tying the pieces of armour to – without the doublet, a man could not be armed.

Armour was put on from the feet upwards. The sabaton was a metal overshoe made from steel strips hinged at both sides to allow the foot to bend. The lower leg armour (greave) was hinged like a book to open over the shin and calf; the sabaton was connected by a lace to its bottom edge. The cuisse and poleyn for thigh and knee were hinged together. They were strapped round the back of the leg, and secured to the doublet. The breast- and back-plates, with hanging skirts, were hinged with pins on the left and buckled together on the right.

Holx a man schaff be armyd at his ese
wsen he schal fighte on foote

He schal haue noo schirte vp on him but a
doublelet of ffisteau sing wrsti sateue cutte
stiff of hoolis. the douwbelet muste be strongeli bonde
there the popints muste be sette aboute the greet of the
arme and the b ste before and beshpnde and the gusse
tis of mayle muste be sowid vn to the douwbelet in
the bought of the arme and vndir the arme the ar
uipinge popints muste be made of fyne twyue suche

A late-fifteenth-century knight being armed for foot combat in a tournament.

Arming a Knight
The following lines form part of a description of the arming of a knight for foot combat in a tournament in the second half of the fifteenth century:
 'First you must set on sabatons [foot-defences] and tie them up on the shoe with small points [laces] that won't break. And then greaves [lower leg-defences] and then cuisses [thigh-defences] and the breech of mail. And the tonlet [skirt] and the breast. And the vambrace and the rerebrace [arm-defences]. And then gloves.'
(From *How a Man Schall be Armyd*)

The arms were covered with arm-guards (vambraces), tied by points from the doublet. Above the vambraces the shoulder pieces (pauldrons) were tied on, and below the vambraces, metal gloves called gauntlets protected the hands.

The helmet was added last, to minimize the build-up of heat. Spurs were worn only if the knight was to ride. The sword was belted on and the knight might also carry a second weapon.

INTO BATTLE

Close Formation
The following lines, written in the thirteenth century, describe how closely packed soldiers beat off enemy attacks at the Battle of Worringen in the Netherlands in 1288:
'The large battle [division] utterly stuck with the duke, composed as it was solely of the men of Brabant, who, fighting in their units, pushed so hard against the enemy – although the struggle was unequal – that neither they nor their leader were beaten into retreat. For they were so well-ordered that they remained together, however hard the enemy pushed them or charged them.'
(From *Rijmkronik*, Jan van Heelu)

In the eleventh century most knights fought on horseback, supported by footsoldiers who included archers and some crossbowmen. The knights charged in groups, following their lord's pennon, throwing, stabbing or levelling their lances. Footsoldiers either went ahead of the horsemen, with archers, to soften up the enemy, or formed a screen to protect the knights.

The knights' charge was difficult to stop, especially when, after about 1100, large tightly packed groups advanced together, all lowering their lances at the same time and producing an effect like a steamroller. At Arsuf in 1191, during the Third Crusade, Richard I used his infantry (footsoldiers) and archers as a screen, hoping to draw Saladin's swift horse archers closer to allow his knights to charge before they could gallop clear.

In the late thirteenth century the Scots tried using infantry with long spears or pikes, forming a 'hedgehog' of points called a schiltron, against which horses refused to charge. Archers could be used to break up these massed ranks of men. But at Bannockburn in 1314 the English archers were caught off guard by the Scots cavalry (mounted knights).

Fifteenth-century armoured and mounted men-at-arms charge with lowered lances, from the Rout of San Romano.

Increasingly, English armies fought mainly on foot, using bodies of men-at-arms with larger and larger groups of archers, all ideally standing in a protected position to make the enemy charge. First used against the Scots, it was a technique that also proved successful in France during the Hundred Years War, producing such victories as Crécy in 1346 (mainly against cavalry) and Agincourt in 1415 (mainly against infantry). But it did not always work – if the English were caught out of position they could be routed, as at Patay in 1429.

By the fifteenth century many men-at-arms only used their warhorses on certain occasions, such as when pursuing fleeing opponents. After the Hundred Years War, longbowmen were ranged against each other in England in the Wars of the Roses. Flemish footsoldiers won a surprising victory over the French at Courtrai in 1302 when they attacked the mounted French knights with clubs and surrounded them. In fifteenth-century Bohemia (part of the present-day Czech Republic), the Slavs in revolt used rings of wagons fitted with guns, and home-made flails, to beat off the armoured knights of the occupying German Empire.

In fourteenth- and fifteenth-century Switzerland, and later also in Germany, ordinary soldiers formed units of specially trained pikemen (infantry carrying spears), who not only stopped cavalry but also fought other pike formations. They became valued as hired soldiers or mercenaries.

A Knight's Ransom
Knights were richer than many other soldiers. On the battlefield they were more use alive than dead, as they could be held for ransom. Their friends and family would pay large amounts for their return. But in the English Wars of the Roses old grudges led to many nobles being killed in revenge.

Late-fifteenth-century woodcut of a German laager or wagon camp.

SIEGES

Surprise Entry

At Château-Gaillard in 1203-4, the French were having difficulty taking the second of the castle's three courtyards. Suddenly, a soldier noticed a disused toilet shaft and climbed up it to let his friends in. They made such a noise that the English defenders panicked and the Frenchmen were able to open the gates for their friends.

In medieval warfare, sieges were more common than battles. Battles were terribly risky: you might be killed or lose your lands. It was far safer to attack an enemy's lands and the manors that tended them. Castles gave local protection and forced an invader to capture each one or leave an enemy in his rear as he advanced.

Sieges were sometimes quite formal, with the besieger's heralds demanding surrender or setting the constable a deadline for a decision. Depending on the strength of a castle or town, the besieger might then encircle it with men, and with ditches or fences, to cut it off from food supplies and stop anyone getting out. If he had time, he could then sit and hope to starve out the defenders, if disease did not break out in his own camp first. Sometimes he built siege castles, structures of earth and wood filled with soldiers, to watch the enemy while the main besieging army moved on.

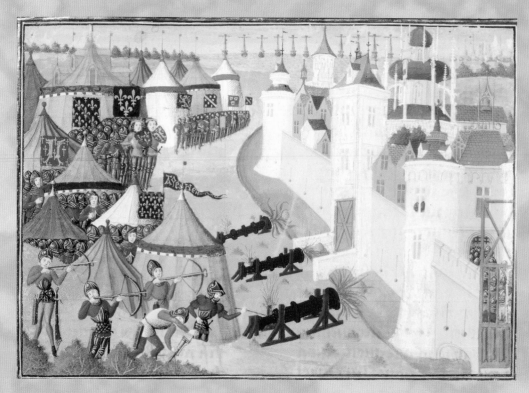

A late-fifteenth-century siege. Cannon are brought up close to bombard the walls with stone shot.

Perhaps the most lethal weapon was the underground mine. The besiegers tunnelled under a wall, replacing the excavated foundations with wooden props. Once the miners were clear, the props would be set alight, bringing the wall down as they burned away.

Battering rams were also used: large tree trunks swung from beneath movable sheds. Missiles were shot into the besieged castle. Some catapults used twisted bundles of rope, sinew or hair to force the throwing arm up. The trebuchet, however, had a large weighted box at one end of a pivoting arm and the missile at the other; when the box pulled one end down, the other lifted and released the missile. Some used a team of men on ropes instead of a box.

Another weapon was the ballista, a giant crossbow that shot large bolts to skewer enemy troops. The ballista was very useful as an anti-personnel weapon, especially when placed near doorways to stop defenders rushing out to attack the besiegers' camp. Using ladders to climb over the walls was very hazardous, so siege towers might be built to launch men across a wooden bridge on to the battlements in groups. But siege towers were slow-moving and could be burned or damaged by missiles.

If a castle or town had refused to surrender and was then captured, the fate of the defenders lay with the commander of the besieging army. Sometimes, soldiers were allowed to march out as worthy opponents, but often the place was sacked and the defenders executed.

Under Siege

This extract describes part of the siege of Exeter by King Stephen in 1136:
'Day and night he perseveringly pushed the siege, at one time mounting the hill with his troops, on horseback, and challenging the besieged to fight; at another causing his slingers to annoy them by hurling stones. He also employed miners to sap the fortifications, and had all manner of machines constructed, some of great height, to overlook what was passing in the garrison, and others on a level with the foundation of the walls, which they were intended to batter down. The besieged on their side lost no time in destroying the machines, and all the ingenuity employed in their construction was wasted.'
(From *Acts of King Stephen*)

Reconstruction of a large trebuchet, its sling lying in a trough ready for launch.

HORSES

Horses were a highly valued part of a knight's equipment. A knight might be busy with his weapon in his right hand and shield in his left, so he had to be able to use his legs and body to control the powerful warhorse. A curb bit, which was like a lever, allowed good control of the horse's head, whilst long stirrups and a high back and front board on the saddle meant a knight was literally standing in the stirrups and held in his seat.

Until the twelfth century, horses do not seem to have been provided with any protection at all. Then, in about 1150, a few were provided with a cloth covering at the front and rear, reaching down to conceal part of their legs. The front extended upwards to form a hood. The cloth probably helped catch weapons, but some coverings may also have been made from padded material. These coats were sometimes made of mail and must have been quite heavy, being worn over a cloth version for comfort.

After about 1200 a few horses began to wear a shaffron, solid protection for the head, made either of steel or of *cuir bouilli*. Such armour remained the main protection and many warhorses still wore none at all.

In the Saddle

The following advice on the use of the saddle in jousts was written in about 1434: 'And in this case I found it good practice, according to our custom, to ride rather upright, with the stirrups long, and having a well-designed saddle: not too wide, not too tight, cut deep where the legs are supposed to fit, and provided with good cushions and padding. The saddle should not throw you backwards or forwards, but should allow you to ride steadily, skilfully and with good control of yourself and your lance.'
(From *The Art of Good Horsemanship*, Duart, King of Portugal)

A thirteenth-century warhorse wearing shaffron and cloth caparison. Note the high saddle boards.

A late-fifteenth-century German armoured knight on horseback in full Gothic armour.

In the fourteenth century, as plate armour for knights became more usual, so horse armour increased. The shaffron might join to neck armour and occasionally a defence called the peytral was strapped round the horse's chest. By 1400, some also had plate armour for the rump.

For the well-off knight in the later fifteenth century, the horse's flanks near the rider's legs might have a plate suspended on either side to fill the gap. This complete armour was very rare, however, and many horses were still given no protection. A complete plate horse armour might weigh about 25-35 kg, and would be lined for comfort.

The Warhorse
The destrier (medieval warhorse) was named after the Latin word *dexter* for 'on the right'. It may have come from the squires' practice of leading horses on their right side. It may also refer to their having been trained to lead with the right leg, allowing them to swerve to that side, away from an opponent on the knight's left.

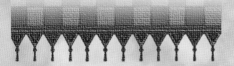

LONGBOW VERSUS CROSSBOW

Speed of Shooting

A skilled longbowman could loose off up to twelve arrows per minute. The spares were stuck in the ground for quick reloading. A crossbowman rarely shot more than one or two bolts per minute.

Throughout the medieval period, the longbow and crossbow were the main missile weapons in sieges and on the battlefield, although slings were still sometimes used. The longbow, especially, needed constant practice to draw the string and perfect the aim. The crossbow, whose cord was also at first pulled back by hand, soon became so powerful that mechanical aids were needed. These allowed a much weaker man to use it – he needed only to learn to aim properly.

A long wooden Viking bow has been found, but the powerful form of longbow seems to have been first used in the twelfth century by the south Welsh. By the late thirteenth century Edward I was organizing large groups of archers, and English and Welsh longbowmen remained a part of the army until Tudor times.

The bow was a single, shaped piece of wood – usually yew from Spain or Italy – that made use of the natural springiness. Provided with carved 'nocks' for the string at the tips, the bows needed a substantial force – a draw-weight of at least 45 to 63 kg – to be pulled.

A fifteenth-century English archer behind defensive stakes. At his belt is a small fist shield called a buckler.

The arrows varied. Wide, barbed heads had long cutting edges for hunting, but could also be used against horses. The bodkin was a slim, needle-like point that could burst mail rings apart. Later arrows seem to have been reinforced with steel to penetrate plate armour. The effective range was about 100 to 300 metres, when a blizzard of shafts could be sent against an enemy as they approached. Sometimes archers stood behind a protective screen of sharpened wooden stakes cut and carried on the march.

A well-armed archer, with arrows stuck in the ground for quick reloading.

Early crossbows had a wooden bow, spanned by pressing the feet against the bow and pulling the cord back over a revolving nut released by a trigger. Soon a more powerful bow of horn and animal sinew was developed, and the steel bow was devised in the fourteenth century. At first a belt hook was used to pull back the cord of the more powerful crossbows, but mechanical aids were needed for the still-stronger bows. These included a lever, a claw that hooked over the cord and was wound back by a ratchet, and a windlass.

A crossbow cord being winched back by a windlass, which used winders, often helped by pulleys.

Longbows Triumph

The following account from about 1370 describes an encounter at the Battle of Crécy in 1346 when Genoese crossbowmen fighting for France opposed English and Welsh longbowmen:
'The Genoese hulloa'd a second time and advanced a little farther, but the English still made no move. Then they raised a third shout, very loud and clear, and began to shoot. At this the English archers took one pace forward and poured out their arrows on the Genoese so thickly and evenly that they fell like snow.'
(From *Chronicles of England*, Jean Froissart)

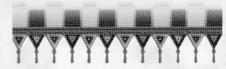

CANNON AND POWDER

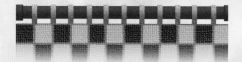

The Bombard

Here is an Italian description from 1376 of a very early cannon:

'The bombard is in truth a very robust iron weapon, having at the front a large chamber into which a round stone the same shape as the duct is placed, and at the back a cannon twice as long as the chamber to which it is most tightly bound, into which a black powder is put made from saltpetre, sulphur and charcoal through an opening in the cannon near its mouth.'
(From *Chronicon Tarvisium*)

It is not clear who invented gunpowder. The Chinese had been making fireworks for hundreds of years and had a recipe for producing bombs in the eleventh century. The first recorded pictures of a cannon in Europe appear in two English manuscripts dated 1326–7. In each, the gun barrel, shaped like a vase, lies on a table and fires a large arrow, apparently with brass feathers. It was probably used against enemy soldiers trying to rush out of a castle gate.

Very large guns were laid on solid wooden beds using cranes. They were called bombards and their purpose was to blast down walls. By the fifteenth century, however, lighter guns were being mounted on wheeled carriages and pulled by horses. Barrels were of two kinds: bombards and some others were made from long iron strips placed side by side and kept in place by iron hoops slipped over them, as in barrel-making; others were cast from bronze.

This bombard, called Mons Meg, was built in 1449. It can be seen on its modern carriage in Edinburgh Castle.

Fifteenth-century Swiss soldiers using field guns, handguns and pikes.

Cannon balls were at first made from stone, carefully carved into a sphere that fitted the barrel, but by 1500 cast-iron balls were coming into use. Other forms of ammunition were being made: shells that burst into fragments, containers that flung out a mass of small pieces against soldiers, or star shells that lit up a night sky.

Gunpowder was either ladled with a long handle, or cloth bags were rammed into a barrel, and fine powder was scattered around the touch-hole. A hot iron or the glowing tip of a slow-match (a length of oil-soaked cord on a forked staff) was then pressed against this powder to create a spark that flashed through the hole to set off the main charge in the barrel.

Handguns were small guns that soldiers could carry, which fired lead balls. They were in use by the late fourteenth century, at first as simple cast-iron tubes with either a metal rod or wooden stock to push against the shoulder to take the recoil when fired. The powder was set off by a hot rod or slow-match, although by 1500 some had a basic form of trigger. Some were hooked over a wall, which absorbed recoil, and became known as 'hook guns'.

Handguns slowly took over from the longbow and crossbow during the sixteenth century. Handgunners, together with massed ranks of infantry bearing pikes or bills, were common in most European armies, which now fielded similar forces. In Spain, cavalry known as jinets were armed with light javelins. Massed pikemen with handgunners and cannon would remain the mainstay of armies well into the seventeenth century.

Loading a Cannon
Some cannon were loaded from the breech, the end nearest the gunner. A removable chamber was packed with enough powder and wedged in place ready to fire. Spare filled chambers could be placed close by for quick reloading.

TIMELINE

1066	Norman invasion of England.
1095	Preaching of the First Crusade.
1099	Capture of Jerusalem by Crusaders.
1187	Crusaders defeated by Saladin at the Horns of Hattin; Saladin captures Jerusalem.
1191	Battle of Arsuf: Richard I holds off Saladin.
1204	Sack of Constantinople by Fourth Crusade and founding of the Latin Empire.
1215	King John seals Magna Carta.
1242	Russians under Alexander Nevsky defeat Teutonic Order at Lake Peipus.
1230–83	The Teutonic Order of German knights conquers and settles in Prussia.
1291	Capture of Acre and loss of Holy Land by Christians.
1297–1305	William Wallace leads Scottish War of Independence.
1298	Battle of Falkirk: Scots pike formations defeated by English under Edward I.
1302	French invading army beaten by Flemish townsmen at Courtrai.
1314	Battle of Bannockburn: English defeated by Scots under Robert the Bruce.
1337	Hundred Years War breaks out between England and France.
1346	Battle of Crécy: French defeated by English under Edward III.
1348–50	The Black Death rages through Europe, killing a third of its people.
1386	Battle of Sempach: Swiss defeat and drive out Austrians.
1410	Battle of Tannenberg: Poles defeat the Teutonic Order.
1415	Battle of Agincourt: French defeated by English under Henry V.
1420–31	The Hussite Wars between the German Empire and Bohemian rebels.
1429	The siege of Orléans by the English is raised by Joan of Arc. Battle of Patay: French defeat English.
1453	Hundred Years War ends and the English leave France.
1454	Wars of the Roses break out in England between Yorkists and Lancastrians.
1456	Gutenberg produces printing for the first time, in Mainz, Germany.
1461	Battle of Towton: Edward IV defeats Lancastrians in England's bloodiest battle.
1469–92	Lorenzo de' Medici rules in Florence.
1477	Battle of Nancy: Swiss defeat and drive out Burgundians.
1485	Battle of Bosworth: Richard III defeated by Henry Tudor, who establishes the Tudor dynasty in England.
1492	Granada falls and all of Spain comes under the Catholic kings. Columbus lands in America.

GLOSSARY AND FURTHER INFORMATION

aketon A padded tunic worn under armour or on its own.

arming doublet A jacket worn under plate armour with mail panels and ties to secure pieces.

ballista A giant crossbow used to shoot at troops during a siege.

basinet A conical or round helmet.

battle A large body of men, forming one division of the army.

bill A farm tool adapted by soldiers for use as a weapon, and later made specially for warfare.

billmen Soldiers carrying bills, especially popular in England.

bolt A short arrow shot from a crossbow.

bombard An early form of cannon used to blast down walls.

boss A metal cup covering the hand-hole in the middle of a shield.

brigandine A coat lined with small plates.

burin A sharp tool for engraving armour.

cavalry Soldiers on horseback.

coat-of-plates A coat lined with plates.

cranequin A hook wound back by a ratchet, for drawing a crossbow cord.

cuir bouilli Leather hardened by soaking or boiling, used to make body armour.

cuirass Armour for the body.

cuisse Plate defence for the thigh.

curie A leather body defence.

flail A spiked bar or ball swung from a long wooden handle.

fuller A groove down the centre of a sword's blade to make it lighter.

gambeson A padded tunic worn under or over armour.

gauntlet Defensive glove.

goat's-foot lever A lever for drawing back a crossbow cord.

greave Plate defence for the lower leg.

halberd Staff weapon with an axehead backed by a hook and topped by a spike.

haubergeon A short mail coat.

hauberk A long mail coat.

infantry Footsoldiers.

jack A padded jacket.

jinet A Spanish light horseman.

lamellar Armour made of small plates laced together.

mace A weapon consisting of a heavy metal head fitted on a wooden handle.

mail Armour made of interlinked iron rings.

mercenary A hired soldier.

muffler A mitten made of mail.

pattern-welding Method of making sword blades by repeatedly folding metal rods.

pauldron Plate defence for the shoulder.

peytral A horse's chest-armour.

pike A very long spear with a plain head.

pikemen Ordinary soldiers carrying long spears.

poleyn Plate defence for the knee.

pollaxe Staff weapon with axe backed by hammer and topped by a spike.

pourpoint A padded tunic worn under armour or on its own.

sabaton Plate defence for the foot.

sallet Type of helmet extending backwards at the neck.

schiltron A formation of tightly packed pikemen, or spearmen.

shaffron Head-defence for a horse.

stake An upright metal bar with expanded top over which armour pieces were shaped.

surcoat A cloth covering over armour that appeared in the twelfth century.

tonlet A skirt of steel hoops.

tow Natural, untwisted flax or fibres.

trebuchet A catapult that worked by counterbalance.

vambrace Plate defence for the arm.

visor Moveable faceguard hinged on the helmet.

windlass A winch for drawing back the string on a crossbow.

RECOMMENDED READING

The Medieval Soldier, Gerry Embleton and John Howe, (Windrow and Greene Ltd, 1994)

Medieval Military Costume, Gerry Embleton, (The Crowood Press, 2000)

Knight, Christopher Gravett, (Eyewitness Guides, Dorling Kindersley, 1993)

The World of the Medieval Knight, Christopher Gravett (Hodder Wayland, 1996)

Castle at War, Andrew Langley (Dorling Kindersley, 1998)

The Best-Ever Book of Castles, Philip Steele (Kingfisher Publications, 1995)

The Best-Ever Book of Knights, Philip Steele (Kingfisher Publications, 1998)

RECOMMENDED WEBSITES

www.metmuseum.org/explore/knights/title.html

www.channel4.com/history/microsites/H/history/guide12/index.html

www.mnsu.edu/emuseum/history/middleages

www.cybrary.org/medieval.htm

http://www.knightsandarmor.com/index.htm

Note to parents and teachers

Every effort has been made by the publishers to ensure that these websites are suitable for children, that they are of the highest educational value, and that they contain no inappropriate or offensive material. However, because of the nature of the Internet, it is impossible to guarantee that the contents of these sites will not be altered. We strongly advise that Internet access is supervised by a responsible adult.

INDEX

A fifteenth-century knight being armed. The vambrace is being laced at the top of his arm.

In the fourteenth century, as plate armour for knights became more usual, so horse armour increased. The shaffron might join to neck armour and occasionally a defence called the peytral was strapped round the horse's chest. By 1400, some also had plate armour for the rump.

For the well-off knight in the later fifteenth century, the horse's flanks near the rider's legs might have a plate suspended on either side to fill the gap. This complete armour was very rare, however, and many horses were still given no protection. A complete plate horse armour might weigh about 25-35 kg, and would be lined for comfort.

A skilled longbowman could loose off up to twelve arrows per minute. The spares were stuck in the ground for quick reloading. A crossbowman rarely shot more than one or two bolts per minute.